Above: Personification of Rhetoric from Gregor Reisch's Margarita Philosophica, 1503. Enthroned in the Roman Senate, Lady Rhetoric is surrounded by ancient authorities: Seneca (moral philosophy), Aristotle (natural philosophy), Emperor Justinian (law), and Cicero (Tullius). The lily and the sword coming out of her mouth represent her power to bring both peace and war, both mercy and judgment.

First published 2015
This edition © Adina Arvatu & Andrew Aberdein, 2015

Published by Wooden Books Ltd.
Glastonbury, Somerset

British Library Cataloguing in Publication Data
Adina Arvatu & Andrew Aberdein

Rhetoric, the Art of Persuasion

A CIP catalogue record for this book is
available from the British Library

ISBN 978 1 904263 90 6

All rights reserved.
For permission to reproduce any part of this
curvaceous tome please contact the publishers.

Printed and bound in Shanghai, China
by Shanghai iPrinting Co., Ltd.
100% recycled papers.

RHETORIC
THE ART OF PERSUASION

Adina Arvatu & Andrew Aberdein

with illustrations by Merrily Harpur

There are many excellent books on rhetoric, including some venerable classics. But here are some recent books that we have found particularly useful: Jeanne Fahnestock, Rhetorical Style: The Uses of Language in Persuasion, *Oxford University Press, 2011; a scholarly and wide-ranging survey of all aspects of rhetoric. Ward Farnsworth,* Farnsworth's Classical English Rhetoric, *Godine, 2011; a detailed look at some of the most useful figures, with many excellent examples. Mark Forsyth,* The Elements of Eloquence, *Icon Books, 2013; a light-hearted treatment of some thirty or so of the best-known figures. Jay Henrichs,* Winning Arguments: From Aristotle to Obama, *Penguin, 2010; an excellent overview, with everyday examples. Sam Leith,* You Talkin' to Me? Rhetoric from Aristotle to Obama, *Profile Books, 2012; a readable survey of the history of rhetoric from a highly entertaining author. Richard Toye,* Rhetoric: A Very Short Introduction, *Oxford University Press, 2013; emphasises the historical context of ancient and modern rhetoric. There are also invaluable online resources; the most extensive is Silva Rhetoricæ at rhetoric.byu.edu.*

Above: 19th century engraving of Demosthenes (384–322 BC) addressing the Athenian assembly. A celebrated orator, he may be best known for his Philippics, speeches denouncing Philip II of Macedon (382–336 BC), the eventual conqueror of Athens. Angry denunciations are still called philippics.

Contents

Introduction	1
The Origins of Rhetoric	2
Enthymeme	4
Ethos, Logos, Pathos	6
The Five Canons	8
Dispositio	10
Kairos; Decorum	12
Epicheireme	14
Metaphor	16
Synecdoche & Metonymy; Catachresis	18
Simile & Analogy	20
Irony	22
Meiosis & Litotes; Hyperbole	24
Sententia & Exemplum	26
Distinctio; Euphemism & Dysphemism	28
Rhetorical Questions	30
Paradox, Oxymoron, & Adynaton	32
Præteritio & Apophasis; Zeugma	34
Concessio; Procatalepsis	36
Repetition	38
Parallelism; Antithesis, Chiasmus, & Antimetabole	40
Alliteration & Assonance; Onomatopoeia	42
Amplification; Tricolon	44
Hyperbaton	46
Wit & Wordplay	48
Epicrisis, Anamnesis, & Allusion; Aposiopesis	50
Pathologies of Style	52
Appendix: Technical Terms	54

Above: La Rhétorique, French tapestry (ca. 1510-1520, Paris, Musée des Arts Décoratifs). The personification of Lady Rhetoric is again majestic—seated on a throne, holding insignia of royalty—and surrounded by practitioners of the art. No ancient or Church authorities are present anymore, reflecting the growing self-confidence of Renaissance rhetoric.

INTRODUCTION

RHETORIC is the *enfant terrible* of the *Trivium* family. Like grammar and logic, it has an ancient pedigree; unlike them, it boasts a rather chequered reputation. At times the infamy even outstrips its ancestry. You cannot, for instance, dismiss someone's speech as 'grammatical' or 'logical,' but let it pack a wallop, and the cry of 'rhetoric!' deafens all. And that is because, from its inception millennia ago, the art of persuasion has been in tension with the truth. And philosophy. For what is to stop a good rhetorician from bending the truth to suit her case? Should rhetoric not make liars and bull-mongers of us all?

The most levelheaded answer ever given to that question remains Aristotle's. Between hard truth and bold-faced lie, he saw a whole domain—known in his day as the *polis*—where things were at best probable. We call it the public sphere, and it is where things need to get done and minds to be made up, where we argue about the right course of action, the most accurate account of events, or the good, the bad, and the uglies in charge of our political fates. If probabilities and values are the main currency in this sphere, then rhetoric and argumentation are its most efficacious tools.

That is why, for centuries, rhetoric was a staple of education in Europe and beyond. It had very useful skills to teach, which helped invent modern English (Shakespeare), steel a country against a terrible enemy (Churchill), move multitudes (Martin Luther King Jr.), or simply communicate effectively. So if you ever wondered about the subtle power that wins over hearts and minds, this little book is for you. And if you never did, it will get you started. For nothing may corrupt like power, but who wants to be powerless in the public sphere?

The Origins of Rhetoric
a charismatic art

Rhetoric began in ancient Greece as the be-all and end-all of public instruction and civic life. Early Greek philosophers known as the Sophists travelled around, offering to teach aspiring youth all they needed to know to succeed in the highly litigious life of the *polis*.

This ultimate art of leadership was rhetoric (Gk. *rhêtorikê technê*, the art of the *rhêtôr*, orator or politician, who regularly spoke in the Athenian Assembly and the courts). One Sophist's name became emblematic for it: Gorgias [ca. 485–380 BC]. Of Sicilian origins, he later plied his trade most profitably in Athens. Of his extant works, the most famous is the *Encomium of Helen*, where he sets out—half in jest—to vindicate the Greek beauty against the charge of starting the Trojan war.

Gorgias examines several scenarios as to what may have led Helen to run away with Paris—fate, force, *logos* (speech), or love—and concludes that she must have been coerced to do so, and hence was undeserving of the blame heaped on her by the poets. The *Encomium* did not clear Helen's name, as it bucked the dominant literary tradition. But it showcased the powers of rhetoric, and Gorgias' daunting skill at conceiving and delivering a seductive, if paradoxical speech. Indeed, of the fourfold argument about the probable causes of Helen's flight, Gorgias retains *logos* as the most powerful and likely one:

> *Speech is a powerful lord, who / with the finest and most invisible body / achieves the most divine works: / it can stop fear and banish grief / and create joy and nurture pity.*

The *Encomium* is a stunning display piece for such dominion. Hypnotically repetitive, rhythmic, euphonic, and metaphorical, it not only tells but also shows how speech, when carefully crafted, can act on the mind like a drug on the body.

Rhetoric's knack for mind-altering effects led Plato [ca. 428–347 BC], Socrates' student and Aristotle's teacher, to start an all-out war against it. His dialogue *Gorgias* marks the onslaught. In it, he denies the Sophists' claim that rhetoric was an art (*technê*), since it was not a form of knowledge, but rather an ease or cleverness with words acquired through experience (*empeiria*). Plato was thus taking aim at Gorgias' historical position that a good politician needed no expert knowledge apart from rhetoric. Then, in an *über*-rhetorical move, Plato compared rhetoric to cosmetics and cookery, all forms of flattery meant to please their ignorant audiences. Only philosophy (Socratic dialectic) could give honest advice or instruction about the good of the *polis*, and is hence the true political art.

And so began the age-old quarrel between philosophy and rhetoric, the latter now forced to wear a big scarlet letter (S for sophistry) on its sleeve.

ENTHYMEME
the rhetorical argument

Aristotle's [384–322 BC] sway over the development of Western rhetoric cannot be overstated. His *Rhetoric* mediates between the Sophists' overconfidence and Plato's wariness by conceding some Sophist points, redefining them, and using them to make rhetoric respectable. He thus grants that rhetoric is an art (*technê*) that can be taught and learnt; more importantly he sees it as a counterpart to *dialectic* (philosophical argumentation or logic), not its nemesis. Both are arts of communication that try to reason their way through difficult human problems with no final answers. Ergo, they are essential tools in situations where such difficulties arise, especially in ethical and civic life.

Rhetoric and dialectic differ in subject (persuasion *vs.* validity), application (matters of practical and public interest *vs.* universal questions), and audience (non-expert *vs.* expert). But their affinity is so strong that rhetoric too should be considered an argumentative art: "Persuasion," Aristotle argues, "is clearly a sort of demonstration, since we are most fully persuaded when we consider a thing to have been demonstrated." He calls rhetorical demonstration ENTHYMEME, after the Sophists, but takes it to work like the *syllogism* in logic, which is a *deductive argument* that draws a necessary conclusion from two propositions (premises) accepted as true:

All men are mortal. Socrates is a man. Therefore, Socrates is mortal.

By contrast, an enthymeme leaves out a premise or even the conclusion if the speaker feels it is too evident (or just plain dubious) to state:

This man deserves punishment, for he is a traitor. Alexander of Aphrodisias

If the glove doesn't fit, the jury must acquit! J. Cochran at the O.J. Simpson trial

If it's Borden, it's got to be good. Borden Dairy slogan

The light that burns twice as bright burns half as long, and you have burned so very, very brightly, Roy. Blade Runner

Because I'm worth it! L'Oréal strapline, (drops the premise and the conclusion)

Enthymemes draw on commonly accepted notions (e.g. traitors should be punished), not logical truths. This does not make them less efficacious. Aristotle's analogy (*p. 20*) explains how and why they work: enthymemes are to rhetoric what syllogisms are to logic—technical means of reasoning from assumed premises to a conclusion. In brief, they are the very body of persuasive proof.

A rhetorical situation has many limitations (social, cognitive, temporal, etc.); it is never ideal. Nor are enthymemes fallacy-proof. In fact, appealing to an audience's pity or fear (*ad misericordiam*, *ad baculum*), invoking an authority (*ad verecundiam*) or popular opinion (*ad populum*), attacking an opponent's character (*ad hominem*), while generally fallacies in logic, are admissible but highly regulated plays in rhetoric.

ETHOS, LOGOS, PATHOS
the three appeals

Aristotle defines rhetoric as "the faculty of observing in any given case the available means of persuasion." He divides these into *technical* (rhetorical) and *non-technical* (extraneous to the art: witnesses, forensic evidence, etc., persuasive means which precede the speaker's intervention). The three technical means of persuasion (or APPEALS) are based on the three key elements of the rhetorical situation: speaker, subject matter, and audience.

ETHOS is your *character* as communicated through your speech. It is an effect of what you say, not of what/who you are. To be persuasive, your *ethos* must inspire confidence, and rhetorical credibility comes from three projected qualities: *good sense*, *good morals*, and *good will*. Absent any one of them, says Aristotle, and you get less cred, which is why attacking an opponent's character, generally a fallacy in logic (*ad hominem*), is permissible and often successful in rhetoric.

LOGOS is your *argument*, covering both the 'what' (the substance) and the 'how' (the style) of your discourse, both the ideas and the words used to convey them. The mark of a persuasive speech is finding in any given case the best possible fit between the two.

PATHOS refers to the *emotions* of your audience (anger, pity, fear, patriotism, sympathy, etc.). Emotions colour judgments and affect outcomes, so to ensure a favourable reception of your *logos*, try to arouse in your audience those emotions that best fit your subject matter and further your cause.

A persuasive speech strikes a fine balance among appeals. Barack Obama's 'race speech,' which won him his presidential nomination in 2008, does

so with great poise. It is, for example, quite common for a speaker to use biography in their *ethos*. Obama does it too:

I am the son of a black man from Kenya and a white woman from Kansas...

But he uses it to tell an 'American story', meant to remind the audience:

that this nation is more than the sum of its parts; that out of many, we are truly one.

This is an appeal to his audience's patriotism (*pathos*). His *ethos* also embodies the idea of racial reconciliation and unity that he argues for in his *logos*:

the complexities of race in this country [are] a part of our union that we have yet to perfect.

But this perfection requires that Americans overcome racial polarisation, so the final anecdote replays this overcoming in an emotional key (*pathos*):

By itself, that single moment of recognition between [a] young white girl and [an] old black man is not enough... But it is where we start. ... [T]hat is where the perfection begins.

THE FIVE CANONS
the persuasive process

Begun by the Greeks, the task of defining the main divisions of the art was completed by the Romans—chiefly Cicero [106–43 BC] and Quintilian [35–after 96 AD]. There are five such divisions (or *canons*), corresponding to the five steps of the persuasive process:

INVENTION (INVENTIO) is the brainstorming stage, when you find the ideas that will help you build a case. To do so, you first need to determine what is at issue (*stasis*, 'conflict'). For that you ask questions of *fact* (did it happen?), *definition* (what happened?), *quality* (was it right/serious?), or *policy/ jurisdiction* (how can it be solved? also, is this the right venue to address it?). *Stasis* theory is a great tool for critical analysis and problem solving. And it's not just for lawyers: relationship offenders practice it with gusto, when they dispute the facts (do you have proof?), the definition (flirting is not cheating), the quality (we were going through a rough patch), or the solution (you cannot break up with me if I break up with you first!).

Next, you have to flesh out your issue by working out the relations that define it. You do so by using rules of thumb called '*topics*' (*topoi*, places), which ask you to *define* and *divide* your issue, *compare* and *contrast* it with others, predict outcomes based on *precedent*, *authorities*, and *language* (general or common *topoi*), or assess its *rightness*, *virtuousness*, or *goodness / advantageousness* (special *topoi*, associated with the three species of rhetoric: judicial, ceremonial, and deliberative; *see p. 12*). If, say, same-sex marriage is the issue, a lot hangs on how you define marriage. Policy issues are generally complex, so you want to divide them and address one subissue at a time (is gun control constitutional *vs.* is it advantageous).

ARRANGEMENT (DISPOSITIO) is next, for a heap of ideas doth not a persuasive speech make. You need to put them in an order that will activate their suasive powers (*for the classical dispositio see overleaf, p. 10*). Jointly, invention and arrangement form the *argumentative* skeleton of a speech.

Then comes STYLE (ELOCUTIO), for "*it is not sufficient to know what one ought to say, but it is necessary to know also how one ought to say it*" (Aristotle). Style is invention at the level of words: it means finding the best language for your ideas. Rhetorical *figures*—the domain of style—make your speech take shape, and are thus the stylistic equivalent of invention *topoi*, which they follow closely. No one style fits all situations, and no stylistic virtue (e.g. the ancients' ornateness) is virtuous with all audiences.

MEMORY (MEMORIA) and, finally, DELIVERY (ACTIO) (intonation, body language) deal with the *performance* side of persuasion. Memorising and rehearsing will help you project confidence and authority, bond with your audience, and respond nimbly to any unforeseen change in the rhetorical landscape.

DISPOSITIO
arranging your ideas

Classical authorities had a clear recipe for how the content of a speech should be arranged: it should be divided into a set number of parts (five for Aristotle, six or seven for Cicero) in a set order. While this structure has often been criticised as unduly restrictive, it is still hard to beat.

The first part is the EXORDIUM (or *prooimion*). Its principal purpose is to establish who you are and why you are the right person to address this topic. As such, it is naturally the place for an *ethos* appeal, demonstrating your character and expertise.

Once that's out of the way, you set out the facts. This is the NARRATIO (*diegesis* or *prothesis*), the basic story that all parties agree on. Of course, since you're the one telling it, you can take the opportunity to present it in a light favourable to your cause, but you should postpone intrinsically controversial material until the next section.

The proper place for contentious matters is the DIVISIO (*partitio* or *propostio*), in which you explain how your version of the facts differs from your opponent's. (Aristotle does not have a separate section for this purpose, which is why his speeches only have five parts.)

Once you have set out the terms of the debate, it's time to show why you're right. This begins with the CONFIRMATIO (*pistis* or *probatio*), in which you offer arguments in defence of your own side. This is where *logos* comes into its own.

Next you turn to your opponent's arguments, and why they are no good. This rebuttal of competing views is the REPREHENSIO (or *confutatio*), another *logos*-heavy section. (Cicero suggests that you may pause at this point for a DIGRESSIO, a sidebar addressing related issues. Later authorities mostly omit this optional extra component.)

Finally, you end on a ringing appeal to your audience's emotions. This is the PERORATIO (*epilogos* or *conclusio*), the climax of the speech. Which emotions you appeal to depends, of course, on your subject matter: compassion when speaking for the defence, righteous anger when speaking for the prosecution, patriotism when rallying troops, and so forth. All of these are *pathos* appeals.

In practice, not every speech need contain every component, nor should all the components always receive equal weight or necessarily occur in this order. The echo of the courtroom and the assembly chamber is audible in the classical *dispositio*, but speeches (and written works) are composed for many other purposes. In particular, epideictic rhetoric (*p. 12*) often calls for a lighter structure—although you could construct a speech of praise with a lengthy *divisio*, in which you enumerate all the reasons people hate your subject, and an equally lengthy *reprehensio*, in which you rebut them, it may be better to pass over such regrettable matters in silence (an APOSIOPESIS, *p. 51*). The greater your experience with *divisio*, as with other supposedly rigid rules of rhetoric, the greater your confidence in knowing when to bend it.

Kairos
& the three species of rhetoric

KAIROS, in ancient Greek, meant the 'right time' or 'opportune moment,' and was always tied to circumstances. It was the crux of Sophistic rhetoric and Gorgias, the world's first pundit, made it a point of virtuoso pride to speak freely to the hour's most pressing concerns.

Aristotle kept *kairos* as a key rhetorical ingredient, but without the Sophists' zing. He put it under a general rule of appropriateness, *prepon*, to occasion, subject, and audience (*see decorum, opposite*). He thus defined rhetoric as the art and skill (*dynamis,* power) of finding '*in any given case* the available means of persuasion,' and identified its three species or branches as *judicial* (forensic), *epideictic* (ceremonial), and *political* (deliberative). Each branch has its own temporal markers: *past* for the facts of a case, *present* for praising or blaming, and *future* for pitching an idea or proposing a bill, respectively.

Tradition embraced Aristotle's solution, so *kairos* now means both the right reason for speaking, and the right tense to speak in. Put proverbially:

To every thing there is a season, and a time to every purpose under the heaven. Eccles. 3:1

A word fitly spoken is like apples of gold in pictures of silver. Prov. 25:11

Decorum
for the rhetorically fit

DECORUM is a general rhetorical principle of appropriateness: if you want to be persuasive, you must fit your style to your subject matter, audience, occasion and goal. This principle applies not only to the style of your speech but also to your style as a speaker: gestures, stance, facial expression, clothing and language, can exhibit decorum—or not. When Queen Victoria complained that Gladstone spoke to her as if she were a public meeting, she was accusing her prime minister of a failure of decorum. But it would have been just as much a failing if he had addressed a public meeting in a manner fit for private conversation.

Yet, taken too rigidly, decorum can breed conformity. And conformity can undermine your character (*ethos*) as a speaker, diminish the credibility of your argument (*logos*), and bore your audience. So optimal rhetorical decorum may call for an occasional dash of inappropriateness, to keep your audience from tuning out. Whence the *paradox* (*p. 32*) of decorum: to show respect for the limits of propriety in the very act of pushing them.

Hence decorum is not just about character. At its best, it is a precise calibration of the three rhetorical appeals (*p. 6*).

EPICHEIREME
& the Toulmin layout

Argument is essential to rhetoric, and often best expressed concisely. Nonetheless, in some contexts, such as forensic rhetoric, arguments need to be made explicit. If an *enthymeme* (*p. 4*) is an argument with something missing, an EPICHEIREME is an argument with extras. An epicheireme comprises five components, usually in the following order: a claim; a reason for that claim; a proof of that reason; an embellishment of the claim; and a restatement of the claim. For example, consider Robert Southey's justification for his attacks on Lord Byron (with added labels):

> [Claim:] *I accused him;...* [Reason:] *because he had committed a high crime and misdemeanour against society,* [Proof of reason:] *by sending forth a work, in which mockery was mingled with horrors, filth with impiety, profligacy with sedition and slander.* [Embellishment:] *For these offences I came forward to arraign him. The accusation was not made darkly, it was not insinuated, nor was it advanced under the cover of a review.* [Restatement of claim:] *I attacked him openly in my own name.*

The most important feature of the epicheireme is that claims should not only have reasons, but those reasons themselves must have reasons (on some accounts, this is all that is required.)

A modern reinvention of the epicheireme is the Toulmin layout, devised by the philosopher Stephen Toulmin in the 1950s. This comprises six components: claim; data; warrant; backing; rebuttal; and qualifier. Here is one of Toulmin's most frequently cited examples:

> *Given that* [D] *Harry was born in Bermuda, we can* [Q] *presumably claim that* [C] *he is British, since* [W] *anyone born in Bermuda will generally be British (on account of* [B] *various statutes...), unless* [R] *his parents were aliens, say.*

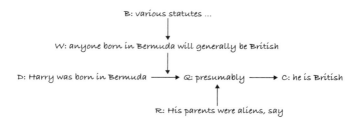

The claim corresponds to that of the epicheireme but the data and warrant subdivide the reason, data being specific to the case in hand, warrant being a more general principle. The warrant is supported by the backing, which loosely corresponds to the proof of reason. The last two components are new: the rebuttal takes note of possible exceptions and the resultant force of the argument is given by the qualifier.

The beauty of the Toulmin layout is its versatility and explicitness: it can be used to make clear (often graphically) the structure and strength of an enormous diversity of arguments.

METAPHOR
life is a box of chocolates

Rhetorical figures may be divided into *tropes* (figures of thought), involving a change in the meaning of words, and *schemes* (figures of speech), involving a change in word order. Tropes are often given pride of place. Indeed, classical rhetoric is a polite establishment wherein METAPHOR rules, IRONY (*p. 22*) secretly contends, and WORDPLAY (*p. 48*) yoricks away.

Metaphors are problem-solving tools, which help us think through a complex or difficult experience in terms of another, simpler or more familiar. (The name comes from the Greek for 'transfer'; *metaphorai* are also means of public transport in Greece). Their function is above all heuristic, or practical, though aesthetic criteria do apply:

> *Love is a kind of warfare.* Ovid

> *Love is a crocodile in the river of desire.* Bhartrhari

A metaphor calls one thing by another's name based on a perceived likeness; it is a comparison between two things expressed definitionally:

> *Life is a box of chocolates, Forrest. You never know what you're gonna get.* Forrest Gump

The comparison's point: life comes with choices, just like chocolates come in flavours. Forrest and most viewers remember this metaphor as a SIMILE (*p. 20*)—"Life is *like* …"—thus shoring up the view that the two tropes part on a technicality (metaphors lack comparison words: 'like,' 'as,' etc.).

But nothing is ever that easy in life and in rhetoric, as the similarity posited by metaphor may be between *relations* rather than things:

> *The hippo of recollection stirred in the muddy waters of the mind.* Terry Pratchett

This metaphor is an ANALOGY (*p. 20*) or proportion: memory is to a clouded mind what a hippo is to a muddy river—a massive, luxuriating, barely stirring dweller. Metaphors have a *tenor* (or subject) and a *vehicle*: 'love' is the tenor and 'crocodile' the vehicle (*see facing page*). Often the tenor is left out, leading to an IMPLICIT metaphor:

> *There is an ocean... And, somewhere in its depths, a Beast, stirring.* Salman Rushdie

We know, contextually, that shame is the ocean and violence, the Beast. They also form a COMPLEX metaphor, as they explore and illuminate each other. A good metaphor establishes connections where none were seen before. Its creative, generative powers are only matched by its expansiveness. Indeed, when pursued for many lines (an EXTENDED metaphor), it can lead to surprising findings:

> *Love is a fire. / It burns everyone. / It disfigures everyone. / It is the world's excuse / for being ugly.* Leonard Cohen

Generally, metaphor is not limited to nouns—or poets: weather is often 'beastly hot' (intensifier); one 'burns' with desire (verb), has a 'cold' heart (adjective), or believes 'blindly' (adverb); plans go 'south' (adverb), etc. It appears language is metaphors all the way down!

Synecdoche & Metonymy
specialised metaphors

If rhetoric is a toolkit, then metaphors are screwdrivers. But, as with screwdrivers, some metaphors have specialised applications. One of these is SYNECDOCHE: the metaphorical use of part for whole, or whole for part:

> *The slogan of progress is changing from the full dinner pail to the full garage.* H.Hoover

> *I do not believe that Washington should do for the people what they can do for themselves through local and private effort.* John F. Kennedy

Full dinner pails and full garages are part of prosperity, but not all of it. Conversely, the whole city of Washington has the government of the United States as a part. A close relative of synecdoche is METONYMY: the metaphorical use of an aspect or attribute for the thing itself:

> *The Red Flag was never flown throughout these islands yet, nor for a thousand years has the flag of any other alien creed.* Michael Heseltine

> *One day you're a signature, next day you're an autograph.* Billy Wilder

Red flags are associated with communists, but are not part of communism. Signatures and autographs look alike, but one is the attribute of a bureaucrat, the other of a celebrity.

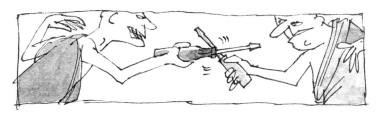

CATACHRESIS
runaway metaphors

Quintilian [c.35–100 AD] defines CATACHRESIS (*abusio*) as "the practice of adapting the nearest available term to describe something for which no actual term exists". The lack of a proper term for, say, the eye of a needle justifies the artifice of calling it an 'eye'. The need to fill such lexical gaps sets catachresis apart from metaphor (*translatio*), which is cavalier towards proper terms. Thus, common phrases like '*foot* of the mountain,' '*head* of the table,' '*lip* of a cliff,' etc., contain catachreses, whereas Hamlet's

> **I will *speak daggers* to her but use none.** William Shakespeare

should be a metaphor, since the transfer of 'daggers' from stabbing to speaking is prompted by the insufficiency of existing proper terms (e.g. 'words'), not their lack. Yet Hamlet's metaphor is also a catachresis, because it is perceived as extreme or 'abusive'. Once separated from metaphor as a form of coerced invention, catachresis is now mostly explained as a special kind of metaphor: either 'dead' (too clichéd and worn out to register as such, e.g. computer 'mouse'), or extreme—a far-fetched, eccentric, mixed, mangled, or even failed exemplar. Something like this sore thumb:

> **... We are riding hell for leather into a health-care box canyon full of spending quicksand, cactus tax hikes, policy briar patches, complete with CMS regulatory rattlesnakes, scorpions, and bad-news bears.** Pat Roberts

The involuntary humour of such runaway metaphors made comedian Stephen Colbert call them 'humaphors.' Here's an intentional example:

> **Hawaii made the mouth of her soul water.** Tom Robbins

For more stylistic fails, intentional or not, see *Pathologies of Style, p. 52*.

Simile & Analogy
comparison

SIMILE likens one thing to another, perhaps incongruously. It differs from metaphor in admitting that it is a comparison—where metaphor identifies two things, simile says they are alike:

> *The stoical scheme of supplying our wants, by lopping off our desires, is like cutting off our feet when we want shoes.* Jonathan Swift

> *To read without reflecting is like eating without digesting.* Edmund Burke

> *Asking a working writer what he thinks about critics is like asking a lamp-post how it feels about dogs.* Christopher Hampton

Similes may be extended or explained by listing points of similarity:

> *Operations of thought are like cavalry charges in a battle — they are strictly limited in number, they require fresh horses, and must only be made at decisive moments.*
> Alfred North Whitehead

> *Trying to maintain good relations with the Communists is like wooing a crocodile. You do not know whether to tickle it under the chin or beat it over the head. When it opens its mouth you cannot tell whether it is trying to smile or preparing to eat you up.* Winston Churchill

This sort of simile is very close to ANALOGY, wherein a comparison is used to reason to some conclusion:

> *Reading is to the mind what exercise is to the body. As by the one, health is preserved, strengthened, and invigorated; by the other, virtue — which is the health of the mind — is kept alive, cherished, and confirmed.* Joseph Addison

> *Confine the expression of popular feeling within rigid limits, surround it with iron bands, and a spark may cause a terrific explosion. Leave it free and like gunpowder scattered in the open air, even if set alight it will do no damage.* Jonathan Swift

Addison's first sentence echoes mathematical usage; it might be rewritten as *reading : mind :: exercise : body*. Indeed, rhetoric borrowed analogy from mathematics. For Greek mathematicians, a *logos* was a ratio and an *analogos* was a comparison of ratios, e.g. the proportion 5:7 :: 15:21. Unlike Addison's analogy, which yields at best a plausible conclusion, mathematical analogies are exact; for example, Archimedes proved that all circles satisfy *area : radius^2 :: circumference : diameter*.

Exact analogies are not restricted to mathematics. They are central to the concept of case law: once a court determines that two cases are similar, it must apply the earlier judgment in the current case. That's how one manufacturer's liability for tainted ginger beer could establish another manufacturer's liability for defective underpants.

Analogy is also a conspicuous feature of much visual rhetoric. Political cartoons often make their point by drawing an analogy. As with verbal analogies, this can be taken too far, leading to visual *catachresis (p. 19)*.

IRONY
the great dissembler

In Greek comedy, the *eiron* was a dissembler who feigned ignorance and employed understatement in order to undercut the *alazon*, a vacuously noisy type, in a battle of wits. Our term IRONY preserves much of this meaning: it implies saying one thing and meaning something quite different, often the very opposite, with the intent not of deceiving anybody but rather of being rightly understood by the right audience. Irony is an intelligence test of sorts, and that is why 'getting it' is very important socially.

There are many kinds of irony: verbal, Socratic, dramatic, situational, etc. Verbal irony is the rhetorical trope *per se*, and the classic form that all the other are based on. At its simplest, verbal irony manifests as **ANTIPHRASIS**, which involves a concise and overt semantic reversal: *Yeah, right!*

Many define antiphrasis as one-word irony (e.g. calling a big guy 'tiny'), but the more important feature is its lack of subtlety. That is why it easily spills over into sarcasm, a bitter-biting-brutal takedown that relies heavily on delivery (intonation, facial expression) for its effect.

Mark Antony's oration over Caesar's slain body contains one of the most famous examples of antiphrasis jacked up to baleful sarcasm:

And Brutus is an honourable man. William Shakespeare

The implication that Brutus is the very opposite of 'honourable' is clearer with every repetition of the phrase, which is used to incite mutiny.

Irony relies heavily on context and often consorts with other figures to make its point. An allusion (*p. 50*) to Pinocchio, say, can suggest that a person's emotional responses are wooden:

Sometimes your movements are so life-like, I forget you're not a real boy.

The Big Bang Theory

Subtle or not, irony bears a straight face. It is why the opening of *A Tale of Two Cities* is often quoted for its masterly use of *anaphora* (*p. 39*) and *antithesis* (*p. 41*), but rarely for its irony:

It was the best of times, it was the worst of times, it was the age of wisdom, it was the age of foolishness, it was the epoch of belief, it was the epoch of incredulity, it was the season of Light, it was the season of Darkness, it was the spring of hope, it was the winter of despair, we had everything before us, we had nothing before us, we were all going direct to Heaven, we were all going direct the other way—in short, the period was so far like the present period, that some of its noisiest authorities insisted on its being received, for good or for evil, in the superlative degree of comparison only. Charles Dickens

The main contrast is not between light and darkness, hope and despair, etc., but rather between overstatement (the hyperbolic claims being reported) and the narrator's understated, ironic conclusion: 'in short, the period was so far like the present period'—read, so very ordinary—that its noisiest authorities were right—read, wrong—to describe it superlatively. Dickens' narrator behaves like a true eiron.

MEIOSIS & LITOTES
understatement

Sometimes less is more. Quiet understatement can speak louder than bold declaration. Together with *hyperbole* (*opposite*), it is one of the principal strategies of irony (*p. 22*). Most understatement takes the form of MEIOSIS:

> I am just going outside and may be some time. Lawrence Oates

A *not uncommon* form of understatement is LITOTES, the denial of a negative term. In this *not unwitty* example, P.G. Wodehouse deploys it playfully:

> I could see that, if not actually disgruntled, he was far from being gruntled.

Like many rhetorical figures, litotes can be overdone:

> I am not, indeed, sure whether it is not true to say that the Milton who once seemed not unlike a seventeenth-century Shelley had not become... Harold Laski

George Orwell was particularly critical of its overuse—it was he who drew attention to the egregious example above. He recommended that writers remember the following to cure themselves of the habit:

> A not unblack dog was chasing a not unsmall rabbit across a not ungreen field.

But both figures of understatement can be effective when used with discretion. Here the two are combined adroitly:

> In my late twenties, it was not unusual for me to wake up in a police cell wearing a paper suit. Waking to glazed tiles and a high barred window, and not knowing how one got there, is a bad way to start the day. Jeremy Clarke

The first sentence exhibits litotes, the second meiosis; together they lend a certain wry irony to an otherwise melancholy image.

Hyperbole
overstatement

Sometimes nothing is so effective as unabashed exaggeration. This is HYPERBOLE. It is especially useful for invective, as in this splendid denunciation of one 19th century Canadian politician by another:

> *He is, without exception, the most notorious liar in all our country. He lies out of every pore in his skin. Whether he is sleeping or waking, on foot or on horseback, talking with his neighbours or writing for a newspaper, a multitudinous swarm of lies, visible, palpable, and tangible, are buzzing and settling about him like flies around a horse in August.* Sir Francis Bond Head, describing William Lyon Mackenzie

The *tricolon (p. 45)* of *isocolons (p. 40)* and concluding simile *(p. 20)* demonstrate how helpful other figures can be in building up a good hyperbole.

As with meiosis *(opposite)*, hyperbole is an intrinsically ironic figure. This can be comic in effect, unintentionally *(as above)* or on purpose:

> *There is only one cure for grey hair. It was invented by a Frenchman. It is called the guillotine.* P.G. Wodehouse

> *If you live to be ninety in England and can still eat a boiled egg they think you deserve the Nobel Prize.* Alan Bennett

SENTENTIA & EXEMPLUM
shared wisdom

Often one's thoughts can best be expressed through the words of others:

> It was prettily devised of Aesop, 'The fly sat upon the axletree of the chariot-wheel and said, what a dust do I raise.' Francis Bacon

Such pithy summaries are examples of SENTENTIA ('judgment')—a.k.a. *maxim*, *adage*, or *proverb*. They express a general truth or commonly held view, and often embody a moral or practical rule of thumb:

> An old saying and a true, 'much drinking, little thinking'. Jonathan Swift

> There is a homely old adage which runs: 'Speak softly and carry a big stick; you will go far.' Theodore Roosevelt

Handed down through generations, maxims are often used as anonymous distillations of wisdom: 'they say…' Few will recall that *'seize the day'* is Horace's, even when they quote it in Latin—*'Carpe diem'*.

Thanks to their currency, maxims are great consensus builders and enthymematic material:

> **O mortal man, nurse not immortal wrath.** <small>Aristotle</small>

By itself, 'it is not right to nurse immortal wrath' is a maxim; but by adding 'mortal man,' a reason is given ('for you are mortal'): the maxim is now an enthymeme (*p. 4*).

Rhetorical *exemplification* (Lat. EXEMPLUM, pl. *exempla*) aims to clarify or illustrate an idea. It is a short historical or fictional tale or anecdote, which serves to reinforce a moral point and get the audience to respond emotionally, not just assent intellectually to it:

> **Old King Tarquin knew what he was about when he symbolised the surest way of enslaving a community by striking off the heads of the tallest poppies.** <small>Lord Salisbury</small>

Not every example is an exemplum. Bumblebee bats and blue whales are examples of mammals, but the story of the dodo—the flightless Mauritian bird that went extinct because it never learned to fear predators—illustrates rhetorically the dangers of being too trusting. Exempla aim for what is exemplary rather than classificatory, and illustrate a moral rather than logical category. Beloved by the ancients and medieval sermon writers, exempla remain a staple of motivational speeches:

> **Americans, traditionally, love to fight. All real Americans love the sting of battle. When you were kids, you all admired the champion marble shooter, the fastest runner, the big league ball players, the toughest boxers. Americans love a winner and will not tolerate a loser. Americans play to win all the time.** <small>George Patton</small>

DISTINCTIO
definition & dissociation

The figure of DISTINCTIO specifies the meaning of key terms. Since so many words are potentially ambiguous, distinctio can be crucial in averting misunderstanding by spelling things out in more detail:

> When I mention religion, I mean the Christian religion; and not only the Christian religion, but the Protestant religion; and not only the Protestant religion, but the Church of England. Henry Fielding

Distinctio is closely related to the strategy of DISSOCIATION, distinguishing two senses of a term that, one contends, have been mistakenly conflated:

> …there are two kinds of equality; there is the equality that levels and destroys and the equality that elevates and creates. Benjamin Disraeli

Although dissociations can be made on many different grounds, they often distinguish between the apparent and the true senses of a term. Asserting that one's preferred sense is the true one is an example of DEFINITION:

> The true University of these days is a collection of books. Thomas Carlyle

This strategy is particularly open to abuse:

> Ordinary temperance is just gross refusal to drink; but true temperance, true temperance is something much more refined. True temperance is a bottle of claret with each meal and three double whiskies after dinner. Aldous Huxley

Definitions of this sort, where the positive (or negative) associations of a term are intended to survive a change in its substantive meaning, are called *persuasive definitions*. This approach is problematic: you may define your terms as you wish, but you do not get to keep all their past associations.

Euphemism & Dysphemism
good and bad names

Giving a thing with a bad reputation a good (or at least neutral) name exemplifies the rhetorical figure of EUPHEMISM:

Other nations use 'force'; we Britons alone use 'Might'. Evelyn Waugh

Sir Roderick Glossop ... is always called a nerve specialist, because it sounds better, but everyone knows that he's really a sort of janitor to the looney-bin. P.G. Wodehouse

Euphemism can be all too easy to see through. If the renamed thing is still seen as bad, then the new term will also soon be seen negatively, so new euphemisms will be required for the old euphemisms, a process known as the 'euphemism treadmill'. Thus the terms 'idiot', 'moron', and 'cretin' originated as euphemisms for older words such as 'dullard', or 'fool', which, ironically, now seem less abusive than their replacements.

The converse of euphemism is DYSPHEMISM, giving something neutral or good a bad name:

There is the milder kind of ridicule that consists in pretending that a reasoned opinion is indistinguishable from an absurd out-of-date prejudice. If you do not like Communism, you are a Red-baiter. George Orwell

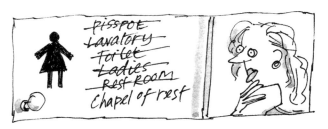

RHETORICAL QUESTIONS
erotesis, hypophora & aporia

Is any figure better known than the rhetorical question? Is there only one sort of rhetorical question? Actually, no: both of these questions are rhetorical questions, but they are examples of significantly different figures. The standard rhetorical question is EROTESIS, a question which presumes its own answer:

> *If you're gonna ask if you can ask me a question, give me time to respond. Unless you're asking rhetorically, in which case the answer is obvious — yes.* Ocean's Twelve

Erotesis is really disguised assertion—the speaker poses a question to which there is only one plausible answer: of course the rhetorical question is the

best known figure! But open questions can also be used rhetorically—just as long as the speaker is sure to supply the answer, as in the second question above. This sort of question is known as HYPOPHORA.

> *What is the best government? That which teaches us to govern ourselves.* Goethe

And here's a neat double act—a hypophora answered with an erotesis:

> *What is conservatism? Is it not adherence to the old and tried, against the new and untried?* Abraham Lincoln

In both erotesis and hypophora we already know the answer when we ask the question. But questions can be used rhetorically even when we don't know the answer. In particular, we can use a question to indicate that nobody knows the answer, an example of APORIA:

> *How many roads must a man walk down / Before you call him a man?* Bob Dylan

How many indeed—who knows? Aporia covers such expressions of doubt, and can serve several purposes. It can be used to suggest that there is just no knowledge to be had:

> *Is there beyond the silent night / An endless day?*
> *Is death a door that leads to light? / We cannot say.* Robert Ingersoll

Or set aside one question to focus on another (an implicit *præteritio*, p. 31):

> *I know not whether Laws be right, / Or whether Laws be wrong;*
> *All that we know who lie in gaol / Is that the wall is strong;*
> *And that each day is like a year, / A year whose days are long.* Oscar Wilde

It can also be a polite way of casting doubt on an interlocutor's words:

> *I know that you believe that you understood what you think I said, but I am not sure you realise that what you heard is not what I meant.* Robert McCloskey

Paradox & Oxymoron
& adynaton

Etymologically, PARADOX means 'contrary to popular opinion,' that is, against the grain of traditional wisdom. Technically, it denotes a statement (by extension, a situation) that seems to contradict itself, or runs counter to logic or expectations. Much like the physics of the Red Queen:

> *...here, you see, it takes all the running you can do, to keep in the same place. If you want to get somewhere else, you must run at least twice as fast as that!* Lewis Carroll

The same 'law' was used in the 1960s to explain economic progress:

> *The United States has to move very fast to even stand still.* John F. Kennedy

Paradox is not a *logical contradiction*, it does not ask us to believe A and not-A at the same time. Rather, it asks us to entertain the possibility that the truth, at least about the moral universe, lies in the tension between contraries. **Without contraries is no progression**, Blake once said, and history may bear that out:

> *Liberty was born in England from the quarrels of tyrants.* Voltaire

> *To be prepared for war is one of the most effectual means of preserving peace.*
> George Washington

A close relation of paradox is OXYMORON ('sharp-dull' in Greek). As its name suggests, it is a contradiction in terms, or a compressed paradox: e.g. *conspicuous absence, eloquent silence, old news, living dead*, etc. Romeo's jeremiad pushes this figure to the absurd:

> *O brawling love, O loving hate, [...] / O heavy lightness, serious vanity, / Misshapen chaos of well-seeming forms! / Feather of lead, bright smoke, cold fire, sick health...*
> William Shakespeare

Sometimes, the contradiction is not apparent until some sharp-dull wit is applied to it:

> I do not know the American gentleman, god forgive me for putting two such words together. Charles Dickens

If paradox and oxymoron are possible impossibilities, ADYNATON emphatically states the impossible, the absurd: *when pigs fly, not until hell freezes over, on St. Never's Day,* etc. Adynaton is emphasis in overdrive, and makes hyperbole (*p. 25*) look like Tom Thumb:

> Build a worm fence round a Winter supply of Summer weather; skim the clouds from the sky with a teaspoon; catch a thunderbolt in a bladder; break a hurricane to harness; [...] bake hell in an ice house; lasso an avalanche; [...] hang out the ocean on a grapevine to dry; put the sky to soak in a gourd; unbuckle the belly band of eternity and paste 'To Let' on the sun and moon, but never, sir, never for a moment delude yourself with the idea that you can beat [Ulysses S.] Grant.
>
> Lt. Col. T. Elwood Zell

Præteritio & Apophasis
passing over in silence

It is often helpful to make clear what you are *not* going to say:

> I will not consider this important topic here and will also make no effort to survey the range of ideas ... that fall within the particular tendency that I will discuss. Noam Chomsky

This is **PRÆTERITIO**. There are many reasons for remaining silent, from limitation of space, as above, to the outright impossibility of saying more:

> Whereof one cannot speak, thereof one must remain silent. Ludwig Wittgenstein

Præteritio also covers cases where the audience's imagination may well outdo the author's descriptive powers, as in this from Lord Salisbury:

> The agonies of a man who has to finish a difficult negotiation, and at the same time to entertain four royalties at a country house can be better imagined than described.

Or the audience may already know the score:

> Biggles tapped a cigarette reflectively on his case. 'You all remember the beginning of this affair, so I needn't go over it all again,' he began. W. E. Johns

Yet Biggles does go over it all again, making his professed præteritio ironic (*p. 22*): such cases of saying exactly what it is that you won't say are sometimes distinguished as **APOPHASIS**. Examples abound in political discourse:

> I won't bring up the fact that your budget has been cut to smithereens, and the Department itself has in many respects been a shambles. Sidney R. Yates

Most masterfully, one may successfully plant the idea one wished to convey without actually, technically, saying it:

> You might very well think that. I couldn't possibly comment. BBC House of Cards

ZEUGMA
sharing a yoke

As a yoke joins together two oxen, so a verb may join together several *objects*, a *subject* several verbs, or a verb several subjects and objects. This figure is called ZEUGMA, from the Greek word for yoke. By making words do multiple duty, zeugma aids concision and points to relationships between the linked clauses.

Zeugma has several subspecies. In PROZEUGMA, the yoke comes first—one verb governs several objects, or several subject–object pairs:

> To be patriotic, hate all nations but your own; to be religious, all sects but your own; to be moral all pretenses but your own. Lionel Strachey

> He would read with that intense application and delight, that he would forget himself, his wound, his confinement, his dinner. Laurence Sterne

In DIAZEUGMA, a noun yokes together a string of verbs:

> They wouldn't even lift a finger to save their own grandmothers from the Ravenous Bugblatter Beast of Traal without orders signed in triplicate, sent in, sent back, queried, lost, found, subjected to public inquiry, lost again, and finally buried in soft peat for three months and recycled as fire lighters. Douglas Adams

In HYPOZEUGMA, the yoke comes last. A verb may connect nouns, as in prozeugma, or a noun adjectives and adjectival phrases, as in this example:

> Desperate, lonely, cut off from the human community which in many cases has ceased to exist, under the sentence of violent death, wracked by desires for intimacy that they do not know how to fulfill, at the same time tormented by the presence of women, men turn to logic. Andrea Nye

Concessio
stooping to conquer

As its name suggests, CONCESSIO means conceding a point, but only to make an even stronger one. Here's Mark Twain in 1902:

> *I am not finding fault with this use of our flag; for in order not to seem eccentric I have swung around, now, and joined the nation in the conviction that nothing can sully a flag. I was not properly reared, and had the illusion that a flag was a thing which must be sacredly guarded against shameful uses and unclean contacts, lest it suffer pollution; and so when it was sent out to the Philippines to float over a wanton war and a robbing expedition I supposed it was polluted, and in an ignorant moment I said so. But I stand corrected. I conceded and acknowledge that it was only the government that sent it on such an errand that was polluted.*

Far from projecting weakness or defeat, concession makes you appear fair-minded and confident, by showing you can and will weigh both sides of an argument. Concessio boosts character and credibility (*see ethos, p. 6*). One author calls it 'rhetorical jujitsu,' since it uses the force of an opponent's argument against them. Sometimes, projecting goodwill and strength of character in the face of defeat is the sole purpose of concession:

> *They asked [Abraham Lincoln] how he felt once after an unsuccessful election. He said he felt like a little boy who had stubbed his toe in the dark. He said that he was too old to cry, but it hurt too much to laugh.* Adlai E. Stevenson

As a 'nay' in the guise of a qualified 'yea,' concession is also an ally of irony:

> *The Labour party is not dead, just brain dead.* Norman Tebbit

> *Your president, President Clinton, is a great communicator. The trouble is, he has absolutely nothing to communicate.* Margaret Thatcher

PROCATALEPSIS
anticipating objections

Your audience will often start formulating their objections long before you've finished speaking. For this reason, it is helpful to anticipate and address such counterarguments, a figure known as PROCATALEPSIS:

> I can think of no one objection, that will possibly be raised against this proposal, unless it should be urged, that the number of people will be thereby much lessened in the Kingdom. This I freely own, and 'twas indeed one principal design in offering it to the world.
>
> Jonathan Swift

> It may be objected, that many who are capable of the higher pleasures, occasionally, under the influence of temptation, postpone them to the lower. But this is quite compatible with a full appreciation of the intrinsic superiority of the higher.
>
> John Stuart Mill

The great strategic value of procatalepsis is that it permits one to frame an objection in terms advantageous to one's argument, and answer accordingly:

> The argument is now put forward that we must never use the atomic bomb until, or unless, it has been used against us first. In other words, you must never fire until you have been shot dead. That seems to be a silly thing to say. Winston Churchill.

Repetition
epizeuxis, epanalepsis, anadiplosis, diacope

Repetition creates connections and patterns, which aid the speaker's memory and the audience's understanding. This is why it is key to many rhetorical schemes. Rhetoricians have distinguished many varieties. Simple repetition of a word is known as EPIZEUXIS:

> Yada, yada, yada! ... Blah, blah, blah!

EPANALEPSIS refers to ending one clause with the words that begin the next:

> Law enforcement is a protecting arm of civil liberties. Civil liberties cannot exist without law enforcement; law enforcement without civil liberties is a hollow mockery. J. Edgar Hoover

In ANADIPLOSIS a sentence begins and ends with the same word (or phrase):

> War can only be abolished through war. Mao Tse-tung

DIACOPE is repetition after an interruption. This example from a legendary master of the pause shows interruption by an epizeuxis:

> Never give in, never give in, never, never, never, never — in nothing, great or small, large or petty — never give in except to convictions of honour and good sense.
>
> Winston Churchill

REPETITION
conduplicatio, anaphora, epistrophe, symploce

CONDUPLICATIO begins a new clause by repeating a key word or phrase from the last:

> Those who have never dwelt in tents have no idea either of the charm or of the discomfort of a nomadic existence. The charm is purely romantic, and consequently very soon proves to be fallacious. Vita Sackville-West

There are also ways of repeating a word or phrase across any number of sentences or clauses: in ANAPHORA the repetition is at the beginning of each sentence; in EPISTROPHE it is at the end; and in SYMPLOCE it's both. Here is an example of anaphora in poetry:

> Then none was for a party; / Then all were for the state;
> Then the great man helped the poor, / And the poor man loved the great:
> Then lands were fairly portioned; / Then spoils were fairly sold:
> The Romans were like brothers / In the brave days of old. Thomas Macaulay

The five *then*'s draw an implicit contrast between the early days of the Roman Republic with the fallen times in which Macaulay's narrator lives.

In the example of epistrophe below, the reader's attention is focused on the inevitability of the repeated notion, instinct:

> Metaphysics is the finding of bad reasons for what we believe upon instinct; but to find these reasons is no less an instinct. F. H. Bradley

Lastly, here is a simple case of symploce:

> Being young is not having any money; being young is not minding not having any money. Katharine Whitehorn

Parallelism
isocolon & parison

Besides repeating words or phrases, you can repeat the structure but change the words. There are several ways of doing this, but the easiest is PARALLELISM, the repetition of some formal feature, some number of times:

> *Some books are to be tasted, others to be swallowed, and some few to be chewed and digested.* Francis Bacon

In ISOCOLON the repeated feature is the (approximate) number of syllables:

> *Kings will be tyrants from policy when subjects are rebels from principle.* Edmund Burke

> *Gentlemen, you had my curiosity. But now you have my attention.* Django Unchained

> *Reading maketh a full man; conference a ready man; and writing an exact man.*
> Francis Bacon

Burke uses two 9-syllable clauses (on either side of 'when'), Tarantino two 8-syllable sentences (excluding 'Gentlemen'), and Bacon three 7-syllable clauses. These passages also exemplify PARISON, a parallelism in which the grammatical structure is repeated. Although isocolon and parison are often combined, they can occur independently:

> *If you think twice before you speak once, you will speak twice the better for it.*

> *As many hands make light work, so several purses make cheap experiments.*

The first of these two quotations from William Penn comprises two grammatically distinct 9-syllable clauses—isocolon without parison; the second line two grammatically parallel clauses of significantly different length—parison without isocolon. Both are parallelisms.

Antithesis & Chiasmus
& antimetabole

Parallelism is a natural complement to ANTITHESIS, a figure that performs the analytically invaluable task of juxtaposing two contrasting ideas:

> The inherent vice of capitalism is the unequal share of blessings; the inherent virtue of socialism is the equal sharing of miseries. Winston Churchill

> The disillusioned Marxist becomes a fascist; the disillusioned anarchist, a Christian. Evelyn Waugh

These examples both exhibit isocolon and parison, as well as anaphora (p. 39)—other figures of repetition can reinforce a parallelism. Parallelism and antithesis may be combined in other ways, such as this *parallelism of antitheses:*

> Education makes a people easy to lead, but difficult to drive; easy to govern, but impossible to enslave. Lord Brougham

An alternative to parallelism is CHIASMUS, in which the second clause reverses the grammatical order of the first:

> To resist was fatal, and it was impossible to fly. Edward Gibbon

> Injustice is relatively easy to bear; what stings is justice. H. L. Mencken

A close relative of chiasmus is ANTIMETABOLE, in which the reverse-order repetition is of words, not (just) grammatical structure:

> Think like a man of action, act like a man of thought. Henri Bergson

> But if thought corrupts language, language can also corrupt thought. George Orwell

> With my mind on my money and my money on my mind. Snoop Dogg

ALLITERATION & ASSONANCE
sound repetition

History repeats itself, they say, because we forget its lessons. Rhetoric repeats a lot, to make things—including history's lessons—memorable:

> Now is the time to make real the promises of democracy. Now is the time to rise from the dark and desolate valley of segregation... Martin Luther King, Jr.

These lines use macro-repetition in the form of *anaphora* (p. 39) ('Now is the time'), but also *micro-repetition*. 'Dark and desolate' is an ALLITERATION—the repetition of a sound, especially a consonant, at the beginning of nearby words in a sequence. Poetry teems with examples:

> In kitchen cups concupiscent curds. Wallace Stevens

Overdone, it can become a vice (PAROEMION) and thus a means of satire:

> Puffs, Powders, Patches, Bibles, Billet-doux. Alexander Pope

Or it can help with memorizing the alphabet or recalling childhoods past:

> David Donald Doo dreamed a dozen doughnuts and a duck-dog, too. Dr Seuss ABC

'Doo' ends with the same stressed vowel as 'too,' illustrating another form of micro-repetition, RHYME, more exactly INTERNAL RHYME (inline).

ASSONANCE consists in the repetition of the same or similar vowel sound in the stressed syllables of nearby words, as in 'fun in the sun,' or:

> On a proud round cloud in white high night e e cummings

Micro-repetitions like these set the tone for the delivery of a speech, and the mood for its reception. And they are highly effective, for they are based on body rhythms—on walking, breathing, or a heart beating.

ONOMATOPOEIA
a zizzer-zazzer-zuz

ONOMATOPOEIA is the kind of name that a thing would give itself, if a thing could name itself; it imitates the sound it names.

> *It's sort of whack, whir, wheeze, whine / Sputter, splat, squirt, scrape / Clink, clank, clunk, clatter...* Todd Rundgren

Onomatopoeia is a powerful tool of linguistic invention, and rhetorically, it is used for both copiousness and brevity. **COPIOUSNESS** (Lat. *copia*), or a great abundance of ways and means of arguing, was the goal of traditional rhetorical instruction. Today, for better or worse, we tend towards brevity, and onomatopoeia zips right to the point:

> **Clunk Click Every Trip.** UK seat-belt promotion

> **Plop, plop, fizz, fizz, what a relief it is.** Alka Seltzer slogan

Add some micro- and macro-repetition (alliteration, rhyme, epizeuxis, etc.), and you get very special sound effects:

> *Once upon a time and a very good time it was there was a moocow coming down along the road and this moocow that was coming down along the road met a nicens little boy named baby tuckoo.* James Joyce

AMPLIFICATION
auxesis, climax, congeries, synonymia, bdelygmia

A critical goal of rhetoric is to focus attention on what you take to be most important. Strategies for achieving this are known as AMPLIFICATION. One example is AUXESIS, the substitution of stronger for weaker terms:

> I have brought before you, judges, not a thief, but a plunderer; not an adulterer, but a ravisher; not a mere committer of sacrilege, but the enemy of all religious observance and all holy things. Cicero

This quote also exhibits CLIMAX, a sequence of increasing force, as in:

> Most people tire of a lecture in ten minutes; clever people can do it in five. Sensible people never go to lectures at all. Stephen Leacock

These climaxes are loose tricolons (*p. 45*), but a climax may have more than three clauses. It is often most effective when combined with other figures:

> [Our aim] is victory, victory at all costs, victory in spite of all terror, victory, however long and hard the road may be; for without victory, there is no survival. W. Churchill

> Peace is a daily, a weekly, a monthly process, gradually changing opinions, slowly eroding old barriers, quietly building new structures. John F. Kennedy

Amplification is the main route to stylistic and argumentative abundance (*see copia, p. 43*). It often takes the form of a list, or CONGERIES. Where the items in the list are synonymous, or nearly so, the congeries is a SYNONYMIA:

> Stop you vandals! You home wreckers! You half-crazed visigoths! You pinstriped barbarians! Douglas Adams

This, as a congeries of insults, has its own delightful name: BDELYGMIA.

TRICOLON
three part harmony

Good things come in threes: somehow, groups of three always seem more natural than pairs or larger groups. This is sometimes called the *Rule of Three*: if you have to have more than one thing, aim for three. In rhetoric, the corresponding figure is TRICOLON, a combination of three related items:

> **A product of the untalented, sold by the unprincipled to the utterly bewildered.** Al Capp

> **She was a woman of mean understanding, little information, and uncertain temper.**
> Jane Austen

Ideally, the three parts of a tricolon should be grammatically identical and equal in length, as in the most famous of Latin tricolons, Julius Caesar's *Veni, vidi, vici*. This is hard to do in English: "I came, I saw, I conquered" doesn't quite make it, since 'conquered' has one too many syllables. Here, a noted tricolon enthusiast comes close to a perfect classical example:

> **Our generation's task is to make these words, these rights, these values—of life, liberty and the pursuit of happiness—real.** Barack Obama (recalling Jefferson)

Hyperbaton
anastrophe, parenthesis, hysteron proteron

HYPERBATON is the generic term for a series of schemes that alter the standard or expected word order in a sentence. Its name is Greek for 'transposition.' In English, where word order is very important for conveying meaning, even small changes can have great effects. Given the standard *Subject–Verb–Object,* or *Subject–Copula–Complement* order, hyperbaton can be as simple as the inversion of subject-object, or subject-complement positions:

> *Clouded, this boy's future is.* Yoda, Star Wars

A small-scale, single-word swap like this is often called ANASTROPHE (Lat. *inversio,* 'reversal'). It is used for emphasis, contrast, or both:

> *Some rise by sin, and some by virtue fall.* William Shakespeare

> *Talent, Mr. Micawber has; capital, Mr. Micawber has not.* Charles Dickens

Anastrophe can sometimes occur as a split-and-swap:

> *One swallow does not a summer make, nor one fine day.* Aristotle

Splitting the verbal phrase 'does not make' and interposing an object has become clichéd as a shorthand argument against generalisation, as it stresses the difference between a sign or property of a thing and the thing itself:

> *Stone walls do not a prison make, / Nor iron bars a cage;*
> *Minds innocent and quiet take / That for an hermitage.* Richard Lovelace

Note also the inversion of the standard adjective-noun order ('minds innocent and quiet') for poetic and emphatic purposes, which is another typical form of anastrophe in English.

HYSTERON PROTERON, or the 'preposterous' scheme (as an Elizabethan rhetorician called it), is also a type of transposition that operates by inversion. It amounts to putting what comes later—logically or chronologically—first, such as the effect before the cause, the cart before the horse, etc.:

> Let us die and rush into battle. Virgil   Find first, seek later. Jean Cocteau

Like *paradox* (*p. 32*), this scheme posits some truth beyond the absurdity (battle readiness is a readiness to die, invention cannot be premeditated). More often, however, hysteron proteron remains a logical fallacy:

> We must explain the force of the horse by the motion of the cart-wheels, and hystero-proterise with a vengeance! Samuel Taylor Coleridge

Other hyperbata disrupt syntactical flow by *insertion*, not by inversion. PARENTHESIS is the most frequent. It consists in interrupting the normal flow of the sentence by inserting some supplementary piece of information (a qualification, description, explanation, etc.), and placing it—as we just did and are now doing—within brackets, dashes, or commas:

> Yours is the Earth and everything's that's in it,
> And—which is more—you'll be a Man, my son! Rudyard Kipling

WIT & WORDPLAY
antanaclasis, syllepsis, polyptoton, paronomasia

G. K. Chesterton once quipped, "It is easy to be solemn; it is so hard to be frivolous." That's because **WIT** is a verbal and intellectual acuity that goes a long way by the shortest route (Aristotle called it "educated insolence"). It is not to be taken lightly, as any Shakespearean fool will tell you: "Better a witty fool, than a foolish wit."

WORDPLAY, the clever or playful use of words, can be witty (rhetorically apt) or foolish (rhetorically crude). Timing (*kairos*, *p. 12*), subject, audience, and goal are things to ponder before using your pun gun. Wordplay is not limited to puns or the four figures below. It also requires you to know your grammar, and be aware that language works thanks to—not despite—ambiguity, thanks to **POLYSEMY** (one word, multiple meanings), **HOMONYMY** (different words, same look and sound), and **HOMOPHONY** (different words, similar sound). If language were a mechanism, ambiguity would be its play or leeway. Witty wordplay uses it to make language do more work; foolish wordplay abuses it, and makes language break down.

Take **ANTANACLASIS**, the repetition of a word in two different senses:

> *...if we don't hang together, by Heavens we shall hang separately.* Frederick Reynolds

The stated *antithesis* (*p. 41*) between 'together' and 'separately' draws attention to the play (polysemy) of 'hanging': solidarity *vs.* execution.

SYLLEPSIS too exploits polysemy, but elides instead of repeating, and makes one polysemic word (usually a verb) govern two or more objects. Structurally, it resembles *zeugma* (*p. 35*), but also stages a clash among the word's meanings, by yoking together cats and dogs, as it were:

> *Miss Bolo ... went straight home in a flood of tears, and a sedan chair.* C. Dickens

Or stain her honour, or her new brocade, / ... Or lose her heart, or necklace, at a ball ... Alexander Pope

POLYPTOTON repeats a word in various grammatical forms (*cognates*). Here's a complex polyptoton, playing off of the basic form '*x*-verb the *x*-noun', with a *double antanaclasis* at the end:

> *There are two types of people: those that talk the talk and those that walk the walk. People who walk the walk sometimes talk the talk but most times they don't talk at all, 'cause they walkin'. Now, people who talk the talk, when it comes time for them to walk the walk, you know what they do? They talk people like me into walkin' for them.* Hustle & Flow

PARONOMASIA, or punning, consists in using words that sound alike but differ in meaning:

> **Immanuel doesn't pun; he Kant.** Oscar Wilde

> **I am General Ising. And he's not an army man, either.** Alfred Hitchcock

Puns use homophony—'can't'/'Kant' (the philosopher's last name), 'General Ising'/'generalising'—and are often *ironic* (*p. 22*), like punning on Kant's alleged incapacity to pun.

Epicrisis
anamnesis & allusion

There are very few dedicated figures of *ethos*, or *pathos*, because any trope or scheme, if well-built and aptly used, will make you cut a good figure, and raise your rhetorical credibility; many can also be used to create a favourable mood for the reception of your argument. EPICRISIS is one of the rare figures of *ethos*. It consists in invoking the authority of past authors, by citing, directly quoting from, and commenting on them:

> *... Archimedes, in explaining the principles of the lever, was said to have declared to his friends: "Give me a place where I can stand — and I shall move the world." My fellow inhabitants of this planet: Let us take our stand here in this Assembly of nations. And let us see if we, in our own time, can move the world to a just and lasting peace.* John F. Kennedy

ANAMNESIS does the same, except it quotes from memory:

> *Archimedes promised to move the Earth if they would give him a point of support ... but in order to move the Earth it is still necessary to build the levers.* Leon Trotsky

Finally, ALLUSION is a passing reference to events, personalities, or sources that are common knowledge in a community. Archimedes' lever was so popular with revolutionaries of all times, especially American ones, that a mere allusion to it sufficed:

> *The good opinion of mankind, like the lever of Archimedes, with the given fulcrum, moves the world.* Thomas Jefferson

The beauty of Kennedy's epicrisis is that certain audiences will have recognised it as also an allusion to Jefferson's allusion, with the United Nations serving as the 'given fulcrum' for world peace.

APOSIOPESIS
at a loss for words

Rhetoric offers many ways to arrange ideas and words, but sometimes silence is just as, if not more effective. This figure is called APOSIOPESIS, and has many uses. Sometimes the speaker simply has no idea how to continue:

> *It's bad enough when the bride decides she's got to join a cult in Devon, but as for this...*
>
> Candia McWilliam

Sometimes it is impossible to continue:

> *The philosopher furiously hurling philosophical imprecations: 'What do you mean you're willing to be irrational? You shouldn't be irrational because...'* Robert Nozick

Nozick's philosopher is in a logical bind: he can't complete the sentence because he would need to give a reason for giving reasons. More mundanely, long lists can trail off into silence when no further details are required:

> *It makes sense to ask: 'Do I really love her, or am I only pretending to myself?' and the process of introspection is the calling up of memories; of imagined possible situations, and of the feelings that one would have if...* Ludwig Wittgenstein

(Is there a trace of *pathos* in the notoriously ascetic Wittgenstein's words?)

An aposiopesis can also forestall a potential disclosure,

> *I sense something; a presence I have not felt since...* Darth Vader, Star Wars

or be used in anger, as in the famous threat from classical literature: *Quos ego...*, with which Virgil's angry Neptune chastises the winds. Literally, this translates as *Whom, I...*, but approximates to Moe Howard's *Why, I oughta...* (or Homer Simpson's *Why, you little...*). The threat is all the more effective (and broadcastable) for not being made explicit.

PATHOLOGIES OF STYLE
words, words, words

Style begins to suffer the minute it takes itself too seriously. When rhetoric omits the other canons (*p. 8*), trusting only in style, it gives up persuasion. The minute style is everything, style is nothing: it becomes mere ornament, often kitsch. In general, over-reliance on style misfires. All figures, if overdone or used inopportunely, can fail. Stylistic faults are usually called *vices*, in recognition of rhetoric's enduring bond with *ethics*. But we can also think of them as *pathologies*, grouped by specific symptoms.

In the *Too Many Words* category, we find style disorders like BATTOLOGY (tedious repetition), PLEONASM (word redundancy: 'free gift'), MACROLOGIA (longwindedness, or Polonius syndrome: see *Hamlet* 2.2.86-94), and TAUTOLOGIA (a failed *synonymia*, *p. 44*). For example:

> I needed a new beginning, so I decided to pay a social visit to a personal friend with whom I share the same mutual objectives and who is one of the most unique individuals I have ever personally met. The end result was an unexpected surprise. When I reiterated again to her the fact that I needed a fresh start, she said I was exactly right... Etc. George Carlin, "Count the Superfluous Redundant Pleonastic Tautologies"

Such disorders occur when amplification (*p. 44*) and repetition (*pp. 38-39*) go wrong, or too far. They often manifest as PURPLE PROSE—first diagnosed by Horace in *Ars Poetica*—and BATHOS (bombast, usually anticlimactic). Such is Signora Psyche Zenobia's predicament:

> What a host of gloomy recollections will ever and anon be awakened in the mind of genius and imaginative contemplation, especially of a genius doomed to the everlasting, and eternal, and continual, and, as one might say, the—continued—yes, the continued and continuous, bitter, harassing, disturbing, and, if

> *I may be allowed the expression, the very disturbing influence of the serene, and godlike, and heavenly, and exalted, and elevated, and, purifying effect of what may be rightly termed the most enviable, the most truly enviable—nay! the most benignly beautiful, the most deliciously ethereal, and, as it were, the most pretty (if I may use so bold an expression) thing (pardon me, gentle reader!) in the world—but I am always led away by my feelings. In such a mind, I repeat, what a host of recollections are stirred up by a trifle!* Edgar Allan Poe

The *Wrong Words* category includes BARBARISM (use of foreign words to impress), SORAISMUS (mixing languages), SOLECISM (grammar mistakes typical of a particular sociolect: 'he ain't'), MALAPROPISM (e.g. Mrs Malaprop in Sheridan's *The Rivals*: 'He is the very pineapple of politeness'), BUSHISM (potent mix of other disorders in this category, not to be 'misunderestimated'), etc.

Perhaps the easiest to spot are the disorders of metaphor, which are induced by overreach (*catachresis, p. 19*), or mixing—wittingly or not:

> **Let your fingers do the walking!.** Yellow Pages slogan

> **[Labour ministers]** *are going about the country stirring up complacency.*
>
> William Whitelaw

APPENDIX - TECHNICAL TERMS

ABUSIO, 19, (ab-YEW-see-oh; L. misuse): = catachresis.

ACTIO, 9, (ack-SHEE-oh; L. doing): one of the five rhetorical canons: delivery; the proper use of voice and gesture (= pronuntiatio).

ADYNATON, 32, (ay-dine-AT-on; Gk. powerless): emphatically stating the impossible or absurd.

ALLEGORY, (al-uh-GREE, Gk. other speaking): an extended and narrativised metaphor, in which agents and actions signify one thing at one level and another at a second, 'hidden' level (e.g. Pilgrim's Progress); often uses personification (cf. personification).

ALLITERATION, 42, (L. much lettering): repetition of a sound, especially a consonant, at the beginning of words.

ALLUSION, 50, (L. playing towards): referring in passing to matters of common knowledge.

AMPLIFICATION, 44, (L. making greater): a general term for strategies that allow you to expand and elaborate on what you take to be most important.

ANACOLUTHON, (an-uh-COL-yew-thon; Gk. not following): a sentence which changes grammatical structure part way through (e.g. 'I Am America (And So Can You)!' Stephen Colbert) (cf. enallage).

ANADIPLOSIS, 38, (an-uh-dip-LOW-sis; Gk. doubling back): a sentence that begins and ends with the same word or phrase.

ANALOGY, 20, (Gk. back reasoning): a comparison (among relations, not things) used to reason to some conclusion.

ANAMNESIS, 50, (an-am-NEE-sis; Gk. reminiscence): quotation from memory.

ANAPHORA, 39, (an-AFF-oar-uh; Gk. carrying back): repeated content at the beginning of several sentences.

ANASTROPHE, 46, (an-as-tro-FEE; Gk. turning back): small scale inversion of the usual word order in a sentence.

ANTANACLASIS, 48, (an-tan-uh-KLAH-sis; Gk. breaking up against): repetition of a word in two different, often clashing senses; a figure of wordplay.

ANTANAGOGE (an-tan-uh-GO-ghee; Gk. bringing up against): 1) the attenuation of a negative point by a positive one—a positive spin (e.g. sure, your glass is half-empty, but also half-full); 2) a countercharge to an opponent's charge (e.g. developing green technologies is expensive, but the cost of not developing them is far greater).

ANTIMERIA, (an-tee-MERE-ee-uh; Gk. opposite part): using non-verb as a verb, a.k.a. 'verbing' (e.g. 'but me no buts'), or vice versa (e.g. 'having a good cry').

ANTIMETABOLE, 41, (an-tee-muh-tab-OH-lee; Gk. turning around): reverse-order repetition of words.

ANTIPHRASIS, 22, (an-tee-FRA-sis; Gk. opposite declaring): single word irony.

ANTITHESIS, 41, (an-TITH-uh-sis; Gk. placing against): juxtaposition of two contrasting ideas.

ANTONOMASIA, (an-ton-oh-MA-zee-uh; Gk. naming instead): use of well-known nicknames (e.g. the Iron Lady) (cf. eponym).

APODIOXIS, (app-oh-dye-OCK-sis; Gk. chasing away): indignantly dismissing an argument as absurd (e.g. 'Piffle!').

APOPHASIS, 34, (app-oh-FAY-sis; Gk. denial): saying what it is that you won't say.

APOPLANESIS, (app-oh-plan-EE-sis; Gk. leading astray): avoiding the issue by rapidly changing the subject (e.g. 'An excellent point, but—do you smell smoke?'). Related to red herring.

APORIA, 30, (app-OAR-ee-uh; Gk. impasse): expression of doubt.

APOSIOPESIS, 51, (app-oh-see-oh-PEE-sis; Gk. becoming silent): breaking off into silence.

APOSTROPHE, (app-os-tro-FEE; Gk. turning away): directly addressing some non-present, or abstract entity—the reader, an idea, an inanimate object, etc. (e.g. 'O Canada! Our home and native land! True patriot love in all thy sons command.').

APPOSITION (L. put against): putting together two noun phrases with the same subject (e.g. 'Sir Robert Walpole, Britain's first prime minister').

ASSONANCE, 42, (ASS-uh-nance; L. responding to): repetition of the same or similar vowel sound in the stressed syllables of nearby words.

ASYNDETON (ay-sin-DIT-on; Gk. unconnected): the omission of conjunctions, such as 'and', 'or', between words, phrases, clauses (cf. polysyndeton), (e.g. I came, I saw, I conquered).

AUXESIS, 44, (AWK-see-sis; Gk. increase): substitution of stronger for weaker terms; a scheme of amplification.

BARBARISM, 53, (Gk. speaking like a foreigner): awkward use of foreign words or pronunciation; hybrid language; a stylistic vice in classical rhetoric.

BATHOS, 52, (BAY-thos; Gk. depth): bombast, usually anticlimactic.

BATTOLOGY, 52, (BAT-oll-odge-ee; Gk. stammering talk): tedious repetition.

BDELYGMIA, 44, (dell-IG-me-uh; Gk. nastiness): a list (=congeries) of insults.

CATACHRESIS, 19, (cat-uh-CREE-sis; Gk. misuse): 1) dead metaphor. 2) forced, extravagant metaphor.

CHIASMUS, 41, (key-as-MUSS; Gk. chi-shaped, i.e. X-shaped): two clauses in which the second clause reverses the grammatical order of the first.

CIRCUMLOCUTION (L. talking around): use of a descriptive phrase to talk in a roundabout way about a topic/person (e.g. 'you-know-who'; or 'ethically challenged' for 'corrupt'), (= periphrasis).

CLIMAX, 44, (kly-max; Gk. ladder): sequence of increasing force.

COMPROBATIO (com-pro-BAH-shee-oh; L. approving): commending a virtue, especially in the audience (connected to ethos) (e.g. 'your kindness obliges me').

CONCESSIO, 36, (con-SESH-ee-oh; L. giving way): conceding a point, in order to make a stronger one.

CONCLUSIO, 11, (con-CLUE-zee-oh; L. shut together): the final stage of a classical speech = epilogos, peroratio).

CONDUPLICATIO, 39, (con-dew-plick-AH-shee-oh; L. doubling up): beginning a new clause by repeating a key word or phrase from the last.

CONFIRMATIO, 10, (con-firm-AH-shee-oh; L. firm together): the stage of a classical speech in which arguments are offered (= pistis, probatio).

CONFUTATIO, 10, (con-few-TAR-shee-oh; L. overthrow altogether): the stage of a classical speech in which opposing arguments are rebutted (= reprehensio).

COPIA, 43, (COE-pee-uh; L. plenty): stylistic and argumentative abundance; the goal of rhetorical instruction in the Renaissance and after.

DECORUM, 13, (deck-OAR-um; L. appropriateness): general principle of propriety, which requires that a speech fit its occasion, audience, and goal.

DEFINITION, 28: asserting that one's preferred sense of a term is the true one.

DIACOPE, 38, (dye-ACK-oh-pee; Gk. cutting through): repetition after an interruption.

DIALECTIC, 4, (die-UH-leck-tick; Gk. debate craft): the art of debate by question and answer; the characteristic mode of reasoning in philosophy.

DIALYSIS, 38, (dye-AL-uh-sis; Gk. splitting apart): a disjunctive argument, in which two or more alternatives are considered (e.g. 'If it moves, salute it. If it doesn't move, pick it up. If you can't pick it up, paint it.').

DIAZEUGMA, 35, (dye-uh-ZYOOG-muh; Gk. yoking through): a zeugma in which one subject governs a string of verbs.

DIEGESIS, 10, (die-UH-gee-sis; Gk. narrative): = narratio.

DIGRESSIO, 11, (die-GRESS-see-oh; L. stepping aside): a digression in a speech.

DIRIMENS COPULATIO (di-ree-MENS cop-yew-LA-shee-oh; L. separating combination): conceding a point, to preserve an appearance of balance (e.g. 'I have the body of a weak, feeble woman; but I have the heart and stomach of a king, and of a king of England too...') (cf. antanagoge, concessio).

DISPOSITIO, 9, (dis-POE-zish-ee-oh; L. placing apart): one of the five rhetorical canons: the arrangement of the ideas in a speech.

DISSOCIATION, 28: distinguishing two senses of a term that, one contends, have been mistakenly conflated.

DISTINCTIO, 28, (diss-tink-SHEE-oh; L. distinguishing): specification of the meaning of key terms.

DIVISIO, 10, (dee-VIZ-ee-oh; L. forcing apart): the stage of a classical speech in which the issues dividing the parties are set out (= partitio, propositio).

DYSPHEMISM, 29, (diss-FUH-mism; Gk. bad speech): giving something neutral or good a bad name (converse of euphemism).

ECPHONESIS, 29, (eck-foe-KNEE-sis; Gk. speaking out): exclamation of extreme emotion (e.g. 'Sufferin' succotash!').

ELOCUTIO, 9, (ell-oh-KEW-shee-oh; L. speaking out): one of the five rhetorical canons: style; finding the best language for your ideas.

EMPEIRIA, 3, (em-PEER-ee-uh; Gk. experience): hands-on know-how.

ENALLAGE, (en-ull-a-GEE; Gk. changing): using one grammatical form where another would be expected (e.g. 'mistakes were made') (cf. anacoluthon).

ENARGEIA (en-ar-GHEE-uh; Gk. clear): set of figures aimed at achieving a vivid description, to reach an audience emotionally (e.g. 'Picture it! Sicily 1922...'); a virtue of style in classical rhetoric.

ENCOMIUM, 2, (en-COE-me-um; Gk. eulogy): a speech of praise.

ENTHYMEME, 4, (enth-ee-MEEM; Gk. in mind): shortened argument, similar to syllogism, but missing a premise, or the conclusion.

ENUMERATIO (ee-new-mare-AH-shee-oh; L. counting out): listing a series of related points.

EPANALEPSIS, 38, (ep-an-uh-LEP-sis; Gk. taking up again): Starting a clause or sentence the same way that the previous clause or sentence ends.

EPICHEIREME, 14, (ep-ee-kai-REAM; Gk. undertaking): an extended argument, with five components, usually in the following order: a claim; a reason for that claim; a proof of that reason; an embellishment of the claim; and a restatement of the claim.

EPICRISIS, 50, (ep-ee-CRY-sis; Gk. deciding upon): invoking the authority of past authors.

EPIDEICTIC, 12, (ep-ee-day-ICK-tick; Gk. showing upon): the branch of rhetoric focused on speeches of praise or censure.

EPILOGOS (ep-ee-LOW-goss; Gr. reason upon): = peroratio.

EPIMONE, 38, (ep-IM-oh-nee; Gk. staying upon): refrain, leitmotif, slogan; persistent repetition of a phrase/word to sway a crowd.

EPIPLEXIS (ep-ee-PLECK-sis; Gk. striking upon): indignant upbraiding, often by means of erotesis (e.g. 'Why died I not from the womb?').

EPISTROPHE, 39, (ep-is-tro-FEE; Gk. turning upon): repeated content at the end of several sentences.

EPITHET, 39, (ep-ee-THET; Gk. placing upon): an adjective or adjectival phrase that qualifies a noun, literally or figuratively (e.g. 'a much-maligned band').

EPIZEUXIS, 38, (ep-ee-ZYOOK-sis; Gk. fastening upon): bare repetition of a single word, with no intervening breaks.

EPONYM, 2, (ep-OH-nim; Gk. given as a name): a name used for the properties for which the name's owner is famous (e.g. 'Machiavellian').

EROTESIS, 30, (erro-TEE-sis; Gk. questioning): a question which presumes its own answer.

ETHOS, 6, (EE-thos; Gk. character): appeal to character; one of the three technical means of persuasion (cf. also logos, pathos).

EUNOIA (yew-NOY-uh; Gk. thinking well): goodwill that a speaker aims to demonstrate and instill in the audience.

EUPHEMISM, 29, (yew-FUH-mism; Gk. good speech): giving something with a bad reputation a good (or neutral) name (converse of dysphemism).

EXEMPLUM, 26, (eck-ZEM-plum; L. sample): a short, historical or fictional narrative used to make a moral point.

EXORDIUM, 10, (eck-ZOR-dee-um; L. beginning from): the introductory stage of a classical speech (= prooimion).

HENDIADYS (hen-dye-UH-diss; Gk. one through two): using two words joined by 'and' to express one idea (e.g. 'nice and easy' for 'nicely easy').

HOMOEOTELEUTON (hoe-me-OH-tell-YEW-ton; Gk. like ending): a sequence of words with similar endings (e.g. 'Got myself a cryin', talkin', sleepin', walkin', livin' doll').

HOMONYMY, 48, (hoe-MON-uh-me; Gk. same law): the capacity of a word or phrase to carry multiple unrelated meanings.

HORISMUS (hoh-RIZ-mus; Gk. boundary): a concise and memorable definition (e.g. 'A horse is dangerous at both ends and uncomfortable in the middle') (or a dissociative definition).

HYPALLAGE (hype-ull-a-GEE; Gk. under changing): an epithet incongruously applied to a noun other than the one it would be expected to modify (e.g. 'he smoked a pensive cigarette') (cf. personification).

HYPERBATON, 46, (high-PAIR-bat-on; Gk. overstepping): group of figures that alter the standard or expected word order.

HYPERBOLE, 25, (high-PAIR-bo-lee; Gk. excess, literally over-throwing): unabashed exaggeration.

HYPOPHORA, 30, (hype-OFF-uh-ruh; Gk. under carrying): answering one's own question.

HYPOTAXIS (hype-o-TACK-sis; Gk. under arrangement): the arrangement of phrases or clauses in a relation of subordination with the help of conjunctions such as 'because' or 'therefore' (cf. parataxis).

HYPOZEUGMA, 35, (hype-o-ZYOOG-muh; Gk. yoking under): a zeugma in which the yoke word comes last.

HYSTERON PROTERON, 47, (HISS-tare-on PRO-tare-on; Gk. the latter, the former): a reversal of logical or chronological order.

INVENTIO, 8, (in-VEN-shee-oh): one of the five rhetorical canons: finding the best ideas and arguments for your case, often by use of topoi.

IRONY, 22, (eye-RON-ee; Gk. dissimulation): saying one thing and meaning something different, often the opposite.

ISOCOLON, 40, (eye-so-COE-lon; Gk. equal limb): a parallelism in which the repeated feature is the (approx.) number of syllables.

KAIROS, 12, (kai-ROSS; Gk. proper time): the persuadable moment, the right time for speaking, but also the right tense to speak in.

LITOTES, 24, (lie-TOE-tease; Gk. small): understatement by the denial of a negative term (e.g. 'it was not unconvincing').

LOCUS (low-CUSS; L. place): = topos.

LOGOS, 6, (LOW-goss; Gk. reason, word): appeal to reason; one of the three technical means of persuasion (cf. also ethos, pathos)

MACROLOGIA, 52, (mack-ro-LODGE-ee-uh; Gk. long-worded): longwindedness, prolixity.

MALAPROPISM, 53, (mal-uh-PROP-ism; F. awkward): comical misuse of words, after Mrs Malaprop, a character in Sheridan's The Rivals, 1775.

MEIOSIS, 24, (my-OH-sis; Gk. lessening): unaffected understatement.

MEMORIA, 9, (mem-OAR-ee-uh; L. memory): one of the five rhetorical canons: memorising what one has to say; more generally the skills of enhancing one's memory.

MERISM (merry-zum; Gk. diving into parts): listing all the parts rather than the whole; a strategy of copia (e.g. 'lock, stock, and barrel').

METABASIS, (met-uh-BAY-sis; Gk. going after): a linking device recapping what was said and previewing what will follow (e.g. '...and with that settled, let us now turn to...').

METANOIA (met-uh-NOY-uh; Gk. change of mind): correcting your own statement to either strengthen or weaken it (e.g. 'one of the best — no, the best').

METAPHOR, 16, (met-uh-FOR; Gk. transfer): calling one thing by another's name in virtue of some similarity or relation discovered through their comparison.

METONYMY, 18, (met-ON-ee-me; Gk. change of name): the metaphorical use of an aspect or attribute for the thing itself.

MYCTERISM (mick-TARE-ism; Gk. sneering): an insult accompanied by an appropriate gesture (e.g. 'Not this again!' <Rolls eyes>).

NARRATIO, 10, (nuh-RAY-shee-oh; L. relating): the stage of a classical speech in which uncontroversial facts are set out (= diegesis, prothesis).

ONOMATOPOEIA, 43, (on-oh-mat-oh-PEE-uh; Gk. making of words): naming a thing with an imitation of its sound.

OXYMORON, 32, (ock-see-MORE-on; Gk. sharp-dull): a contradiction in terms or compressed paradox.

PARADOX, 32, (pa-ra-DOCKS; Gk. contrary to received opinion): apparent self-contradiction, or anything running counter to logic or expectations.

PARALLELISM, 40, (pa-ra-lell-ism; Gk. beside one another): the repetition of some formal feature, some number of times.

PARATAXIS (pa-ra-TACK-sis; Gk. alongside arrangement): the opposite of hypotaxis; juxtaposition of clauses or phrases without subordinating conjunctions.

PARENTHESIS, 47, (pa-renth-UH-sis; Gk. placing beside): a species of hyperbaton that interrupts one sentence with another (or with a word or phrase).

PARISON, 40, (pa-rees-ON; Gk. exactly balanced): a parallelism in which the grammatical structure is repeated.

PAROEMION, 42, (pa-REE-me-on; Gk. near like): overdone alliteration.

PARONOMASIA, 48, (pa-ro-no-MA-zee-uh; Gk. naming beside): punning.

PARTITIO, 10, (par-TISH-ee-oh; L. dividing into parts): the stage of a classical speech in which the issues dividing the parties are set out (= divisio, propostio).

PATHOS, 6, (PAY-thos; Gk. feeling): appeal to emotions; one of the three technical means of persuasion (cf. also ethos, logos).

PERIPHRASIS (perry-FRA-sis; Gr. round about declaring): = circumlocution.

PERORATIO, 11, (perro-RAY-shee-oh; L. speaking through): the final stage of a classical speech (= conclusio, epilogos).

PERSONIFICATION: the ascription of human attributes, such as emotions, to inanimate objects or abstract entities (e.g. 'gloomy clouds threatened miserable rain'), (= prosopopoeia).

PERSUASIVE DEFINITION, 28: a definition where positive (or negative) prior associations are intended to survive a change in substantive meaning.

PHILIPPIC (fill-LIP-ick; Gk. concerning Philip): a speech of bitter invective, after Demosthenes's attacks on Philip II of Macedon.

PHRONESIS (fro-KNEE-sis; Gk. thinking): practical wisdom or prudence; for Aristotle the faculty of knowing what one ought to do and how to achieve it; good sense as projected by the speaker in an ethos appeal.

PISTIS, 10, (PISS-tiss; Gk. belief): = confirmatio.

PLEONASM, 52, (PLEA-on-asm; Gk. superfluity): use of redundant words.

POLIS (POE-liss; Gk. city): names the form of political organisation (city-state) in ancient Greece; by extension, the community of discourse, or public sphere, in which rational debate occurs.

POLYPTOTON, 48, (pol-ip-TOE-ton; Gk. *many falling*): repetition of a word in different grammatical forms.

POLYSEMY, 48, (pol-ee-SEE-me; Gk. *many signs*): the capacity of a word or phrase to carry multiple related meanings. (cf. homonymy).

POLYSYNDETON (pol-ee-sind-IT-on; Gk. *many binding*): the use of unnecessary conjunctions between words or phrases or clauses (e.g. 'East and west and south and north/The messengers ride fast').

PRÆTERITIO, 34, (pritt-air-ISH-ee-oh; L. *passing over*): giving reasons for remaining silent.

PROBATIO (pro-BAH-shee-oh; L. *proving*): = confirmatio.

PROCATALEPSIS, 37, (pro-cat-UH-lep-sis; Gk. *taking up beforehand*): anticipating and addressing counterarguments.

PROLEPSIS (PRO-lep-sis; Gk. *preconception*): use of an epithet before it is strictly applicable (e.g. 'I bet on the losing horse'), (or = procatalepsis).

PRONUNTIATIO (pro-nun-shee-AH-shee-oh; L. *announcing forth*) = actio.

PROOIMION, 10, (pro-OI-me-on; Gk. *prelude*; Latinised as procemium or proem): = exordium.

PROPOSITIO, 10, (prop-oh-ZISH-ee-oh; L. *setting forth*): = divisio

PROSOPOPOEIA (pro-soh-poh-PEE-uh, Gk. *making face*): = personification.

PROTHESIS, 10, (prowth-EE-sis; Gk. *placing before*): = narratio.

PROZEUGMA, 35, (pro-ZYOOG-muh; Gk. *yoking before*): a zeugma in which the yoke word comes first—one verb governs several objects, or several subject–object pairs.

REPREHENSIO, 10, (rep-ree-HEN-see-oh; L. *seizing back*): the stage of a classical speech in which opposing arguments are rebutted (= confutatio).

RHETOR, 2, (RAY-tor; Gk. *orator*): a practitioner of rhetoric; a skilful speaker or arguer.

SCESIS ONOMATON (SKEE-sis oh-NO-mat-on; Gk.*relation of words*): a sequence of verbless phrases (e.g. 'A man, a plan, a canal—Panama!').

SENTENTIA, 26, (sen-ten-SHA; L. *maxim*): a short and pithy formulation (also known as maxim, adage, proverb).

SIMILE, 20, (sim-ill-EE; L. *like*): explicitly likening one thing to another, perhaps incongruously.

SOLECISM, 53, (sol-UH-sism; Gk. *speaking incorrectly*): Incorrect grammatical form, sometimes used for great effect (e.g. 'ain't' and double negation in hip-hop).

SORAISMUS, 53, (soh-ray-is-MUSS; Gk. *falling in a heap*): heaping up of foreign expressions from multiple languages, often humorous.

STASIS, 8, (STAY-sis; Gk. *standing*): the matter at issue in a debate, or a procedure for discovering it.

SYLLEPSIS, 48, (sill-EP-sis; Gk. *taking together*): using one word in two or more senses to govern incongruous objects (cf. zeugma).

SYLLOGISM, 4, (sill-ODGE-ism; Gk. *reasoning together*): a deductive argument that draws a necessary conclusion from two premises.

SYMPLOCE, 39, (sim-PLOH-see; Gk. *interweaving*): repeated content at the beginning and end of several sentences.

SYNECDOCHE, 18, (sin-eck-DOE-kee; Gk. *taking with something else*): the metaphorical use of part for whole, or whole for part.

SYNONYMIA, 44, (sin-oh-NIM-ee-uh; Gk.*naming alike*): a sequence of synonyms (cf. congeries).

SYSTROPHE (sis-tro-FEE; Gk. *turning together*): indirect definition by enumeration of properties (e.g. 'Quadruped. Graminivorous. Forty teeth, namely twenty-four grinders, four eye-teeth, and twelve incisive...') (cf. horismus).

TAUTOLOGIA, 52, (taw-toe-LODGE-ia; Gk. *saying the same*): tedious repetition of the same idea in different words; failed synonymia.

TECHNÈ (TECK-nay; Gk. *craft*): a practical skill.

TENOR, 17, (TEN-uh; L. *that which holds*): the subject of a metaphor, whether expressed or not; that which a metaphor refers to (cf. vehicle).

TOPOS, 8, (TOE-poss; Gk. *place*): one of a number of generic argument patterns, adaptable for specific circumstances (= locus).

TRANSLATIO, 19, (trans-LA-shee-oh; L. *carrying across*): = metaphor.

TRICOLON, 45, (try-COE-lon; Gk. *three limbs*): a series of three phrases/clauses, of roughly the same length and grammatical structure.

VEHICLE, 17, (L. *carrier*): the image that carries the weight of the comparison in a metaphor; that which the tenor is compared to (cf. tenor).

ZEUGMA, 35, (ZYOOG-muh; Gk. *yoking*): using one word to govern two or more objects (cf. syllepsis).